G000168459

FAMOUS ON INSTAGRAM

Practical tips to make you attractive NOW

Susan Howard

Why I wrote this book?

It looks that Instagram is the most popular social media today. I've just been in a big event with more than 100 people around me. After some time, more than half of them were looking at their phones. It was so obvious that majority of them is on Instagram. They (including me) want to share where they are at the moment and to get recognition or even make some people jealous.

While some generations do not understand the obsession with Instagram, many people would like to be famous and to have hundreds of thousands "friends." Moreover, when we see that some people made serious amount of money and carrier: thanks to Instagram, that they get 50 comments for some simple photo from the beach. We want the same. It is human to start thinking – why not me? "I am better, and I have more to offer."

I wrote this book to help you practically to do everything to have a perfect presence on Instagram. I guess that you already know a lot, but you need to know everything and to decide how to do some things to be successful on Instagram. Practical tips in this book will help you with that.

If you want to read more free tips on use of social media and other aspects of modern and urban life, please visit: www.urbanlife.tips

Why should you read this book?

I don't know anyone who read results of research and expert advice before signing up on Instagram. All of us did it spontaneously and learned what is good and what is bad over the time. However, you are probably curious why some people are more successful on Instagram than you - What they do differently and why their posts are well-received by their friends. Why some of them have hundreds of thousands of followers, and you have less than 100.

One of the key reasons to read this book is because you need to understand that there is no difference between "business profile" and your "personal profile" if you want to become well-known and famous. Your funs are your clients. You are brand. Consequently, in the book, I am using terms "business," "client," "product," "brand" because I want to remind you on it and make you start thinking about yourself on Instagram from a business perspective. That is the most important thing you should know before start reading this book.

You will find all answers here including pros and cons for some alternatives and learn how to improve your presence dramatically. Yes, you can be famous or at least well-known for quite a short amount of time.

TABLE OF CONTENT

INTRODUCTION

I'm not going to ask why you want to be famous in the first place. That might end up being a too philosophic conversation and it's a topic for another time. But if you do, then here's why you should consider Instagram.

Instagram is a simple way to capture and share the world's moments. Follow your friends and family to see what they're up to, and discover accounts from all over the world that are sharing things you love.

In the quaint old days of 2012, $1 billion was an eye-popping sum to pay for a startup, especially one that made no money and had just 13 full-time employees. So when Facebook agreed to buy Instagram for that amount, some observers were left scratching their heads.

Four years later, it's obvious: At $1 billion, Instagram was a steal and one of the smartest acquisitions ever in consumer tech. (Though $1 billion was the headline price, the final acquisition closed at $715 million due to a decline in the value of Facebook's stock.)

Instagram had just 30 million users when it was bought two years after its 2010 launch. Today the photo-sharing app has more than 400 million users, eclipsing even Twitter. Facebook is likely hoping Instagram can grow into its fourth billion-user platform, after Facebook itself, WhatsApp (also an acquisition) and Messenger. Even if it doesn't reach the heights of Facebook's other properties, Instagram is already the biggest revenue driver for the company outside of its flagship app. After slowly rolling out highly curated ads, Instagram finally opened the floodgates last fall by allowing anyone to advertise on the platform.

Who wouldn't? Having a luxurious life of traveling the world, meeting with other famous and inspirational people, being adored and the list goes on. Sounds good, doesn't it?

So Yes, It Makes Sense to Be Present On Instagram.

CHAPTER ONE

HOW TO HAVE INTERESTING PROFILE

Having interesting profile is a key step if you want to be famous on the internet. Many easy steps could not be skipped, and some of them must be done carefully. You don't have to be IT or marketing experts. Just think about each of steps in this list and if you want to know more, subscribe to my FREE newsletter at www.urbanlife.tips/free

Basic steps

> STEP 1: *Choose a Brand-centric Username*

This should be a no-brainer, but try to use a decent business username. Besides being relevant, a unique username will stick with the followers. Another tip is to make your username consistent across all your social media platforms. It acts as a recognizable 'brand identity' and is easier for people to search. They will know that it is the 'real' you or business right away. Changing your display name is very easy on Instagram. However, try not to change it as and when you like as doing so would rock the confidence of your followers. If you really have to change your social media names for some reason, always remember that your username is your brand!

➤ STEP 2: *Personality Rich Profile Photo*

Your profile picture might be the first thing that potential followers will look at besides the username. So do keep in mind how you would like your viewers to think of you. While a professional looking photo like the ones you use in your résumé may be good, they can be a tad bit boring. Inject some of your personality in your profile photo – be creative, unique and recognizable in your profile picture. Another handy tip is to stick to your business logo if you have one.

➤ STEP 3: *Short but Relevant Bio*

An Instagram bio does have its word limit. Remember to keep it short and straight to the point. Here are five things you need to consider:

- Tell viewers who you are.
- Explain what you can do or are doing.
- State, your topic of influence on Instagram, be it lifestyle, fitness, food, fashion or others.
- State where you come from.

➤ STEP 4: *Use Right Blend of Hashtags*

Hashtags are all about creating the buzz for your brand so unleash your creativity and have fun. Create the awareness you need by doing the following:

- Use generic hashtags – #fashion, #alcohol, #beverage
- Use up to a total of approximately ten to 12 hashtags
- Create personalized hashtags with relevance to what you are promoting you or your business

➤ STEP 5: *Follow The Right Frequency Of Posts*

There are no rules as to how many times you should post on Instagram, as it will not turn your followers away.

Unsurprisingly, not updating frequently causes a drop in the follower counts. However, as a rule of thumb, it would be good to minimally post at least once a day or once every two days, especially during the "growth phase" of your Instagram account. Always make sure you have all your interesting and engaging posts ready for sharing! I will teach you what interesting post on Instagram is. Don't worry!

➢ STEP 6: *Get Your Instagram Photos* Noticed

Once you've uploaded some really good photos and made your profile look interesting, it's time to attract everyone's attention. Your aim is to get more Instagram followers, as well as more likes and comments on your photos.

➢ STEP 7: *Engage With Your Instagram Followers*

While everyone gets obsessed with the number of followers, keeping your followers happy and engaged is equally important if you want to build a relationship with them and get the most out of your Instagram experience. Your bio - make the most of it

Your bio – make the most of it

Many young people think that "bio" is not applicable to them since they don't have anything to offer. That is completely wrong since all logic that companies implement for business is fully applicable for personal profiles too.

Tip #1: *Your name*

The first step to creating good Instagram bios is making sure that your name is, in fact, your name! People searching for you on Instagram will likely use your name (or your company's name), and consistency lets people know that the Instagram profile they're viewing actually belongs to you and not an impostor of fake account.

Tip #2: *Your skills*

A good Instagram bio accurately explains who are you or what your business is and what you do. So if you want to stand out for a particular skill, profession, hobby, or interest, you should include these details in your Instagram bio as well! If you are a student and not doing anything particular, you are selling your lifestyle and you as a person.

Tip #3: *Keywords*

Using keywords won't improve your searchability on Instagram but it will give your account more focus. When deciding what keywords to include in your Instagram bio, try to think about both your core values and the core values of your target audience.

Tip #4: *You're Email*

While adding a link to your website in your Instagram bio is ALWAYS a good idea, it's also becoming more common for users to share their email in their Instagram bio.

So, you have your Instagram account. Now What?

If you want to drive engagement on Instagram, there's plenty you can do to increase your visibility to get more likes, comments and followers.

Getting engagement on Instagram

Tip #1: *Include Clear Calls to Action*

On Instagram, calls to action (CTAs) appear either in the image itself or the caption. For example, tea and juice brand *Brisk* has the like built into the CTA. The company asks fans to double-tap their favourite flavor. Famous people on Instagram are doing the same. As you know, any double-tap on the image will result in a like.

Tip #2: *Use Location for Calls to Action*

Since Instagram only allows advertisers to share a clickable link in their posts, adding text to location is a great workaround to highlights a call to action. For example, in the highly visible location spot, someone tells their followers to goes to the "link in our profile" to be a featured Photo of the Day.

Tip #3: *Leverage Relevant Hashtags*

Hashtags are a great way for brands to stand out on Instagram and find people who are not yet following their account. Hashtags help organize and categorize images and video content, which aids in the process of content discovery. Just make sure to use Instagram hashtags that are relevant to the audience you're attempting to reach. With proper hashtags, you will get a lot of followers, and that is why I will remind you of them at so many places in this book. Again, #hashtag!

Tip #4: *Do Shout-outs for Shout-outs*

On Instagram, you might notice people commenting on your photos with the acronym S4S, which stands for shout-out for shout-out. A shout-out is when you promote someone else's account to your own followers.

Tips #5: *Vary Caption Length*

While Instagram is primarily considered a photo sharing application, some brands or people use it as a platform for sharing the written word. Each Instagram post allows 2,000 characters for captions, so why not push the limits and try something different?

Tip #6: *Interact With Other Users' Content*

Don't just use hashtags to distribute content more effectively; also use them to find like-minded users who do the same thing.

For example, if you're in the fitness industry, search for hashtags like #Fitspiration or Fitness Addict. Then engage with users who are sharing content with this tag.

Tip #7: *Promote Your Account on Other Networks*

After you've established a nice presence on Instagram with lots of quality content, share your posts on other platforms. It's an excellent way to encourage new people to follow you on Instagram.

Promote your Instagram account on other channels such as Twitter, Facebook, and even Snapchat. Get creative with your Instagram marketing. In addition to sharing your Instagram account name or URL, give users a sample of the great content they will only find on Instagram.

Getting Followers

What might Instagram users consider when they decide whether to follow you? Chances are good that they'll check out your profile first. To that end, if you want to get followers on Instagram, be sure you have completed your profile with a profile picture, a description, and a link to your website.

What's more is that you want the photos themselves to look complete and professional. Instagram's header section is composed of seven of your most popular images. Be sure that you've taken at least seven images before you begin promoting your profile. Lifestyle and personal images tend to do best.

CHAPTER TWO

MAKING AMAZING POSTS

Instagram is another web-based social networking stage like Facebook and Twitter, except for that it just enables you to post pictures and recordings through enlisted accounts. Not certain what to post on Instagram today, or can't think what to plan this week? You heedlessly look through your camera move for something, anything, and everything you can see is one million photographs. Not precisely the stuff of a rousing Instagram encourages.

A Few Of The Thoughts You Can Make Astounding Posts On Instagram:

- What you had for breakfast
- Your outfit
- Blossoms
- Make a custom realistic
- Make an inquiry

Photos

To develop your effect on Instagram and for you to champion, you must continually post pictures that fit with your image or subject and anything that features your innovativeness or uniqueness.

Instagram makes it simple to make and offer incredible looking photographs with your cell phone. To take a photograph, tap the Camera catch, at that point tap the Shutter catch. Applying a channel: After you've taken a photograph, you can apply a channel to give it a fascinating look and feel. Sharing the photograph: When you're set, tap Next. You would then be able to include an inscription, share with other interpersonal organizations.

Get Descriptive

Photograph without subtitles resembles book without a title. You may have the correct photograph, however, communicating your emotions behind it assume significant part in your general association with the photograph. Individuals search for the photograph and after that read the subtitle to comprehend the setting behind it.

Approve Photo Tags Before The Content Shows On Your Profile

Today Instagram dispatches photograph labelling, the component that powered Facebook's initial development. New Instagram iOS and Android refreshes taking off now let you label any individual or brand in your own photographs, which at that point naturally appear in the "Photographs of You" area of their profile. You can either label somebody before composing content about your photo or after composing content about your photo. You get told when you when you're labelled, can require endorsements before photographs hit your profile, and have the choice to tag yourself.

A Photo A Day

Photograph challenges the various topics that arise on Instagram consistently, reassuring individuals to take more photographs, boosting our imagination and expanding our lives. The ideal approach to praise the fruition of a photo challenge is for transforming the recollections into an excellent photograph book with the photos from your hashtag ventures.

Ask Friends To Help You With Photos

Regardless of whether you're on Instagram for business or joy, everybody needs more adherents and it's not only for vanity; it's a great business. Instagram has rapidly turned out to be a standout amongst the most mainstream web-based social networking stages, with more than 200 million dynamic months to month clients. It's incredible for systems administration, constructing a following and sharing substance.

Videos

Instagram is a perfect stage for sharing outwardly convincing stories. A video, in any case, is justified regardless of a thousand pictures. Instagram is best known for photographs, yet recordings have been a gigantic hit on this portable stage. When your present recordings on Instagram identified with your business or you, you are exploiting portable but effective advertising.

Instagram recordings make two times more commitment by and large than Instagram photographs do. They likewise have a higher rate of offers on Twitter and different stages.

There are three (obvious) ways to use Instagram video:

- Offer limited-time offers
- Demonstrate your products in real life
- Welcome an Influencer to take over your story

Apps to create videos on Instagram

Over five million businesses around the world use Instagram to tell their story. With this much competition, it's clear your brand needs to find new ways to stand out. Thankfully, there are Instagram apps that can help. To save you time, we've rounded up 14 of the best apps out there. The best Instagram apps that will help you with videos (and photos):

- Layout
- Hootsuite Enhance
- Have 2 Have It
- Boomerang
- Hootsuite Campaigns App
- Hyper-Lapse
- Pic Stitch
- Microsoft Selfie
- HootSuite (dashboard or mobile app)
- When to Post
- Swipeable

Bonus application: Watermark Video Square Free

If you want to protect your video, you can use an application such as Watermark Video Square to easily protect your video with your own text watermark. This will avoid scammer reposting, and your fans will like it. Simply add "@Username," "Copyright © YOUR TEXT," "Trademark™," "#Hashtag,"

"Signature," "@Email" or text for personal, professionals and business use. Claim your rights before your video or artwork goes viral.

Important Video marketing practices on Instagram

Use "square" or 1:1 format

Studies show it costs 33% less to get someone to engage with square video (source)

Think "no sound."

Instagram requires that you "tap video for sound" meaning silence is automatic (source)

Aim to keep your videos on par with your photos

Both photos and videos from the same location and situation are always good ideas.

Hashtags again

Posts with at least one hashtag get 12% more engagement. Remember to optimize captions & tags.

Instagram Stories allows uploading of videos within 24 hours of being "added" to your phone. Anything you create on your computer and send to your phone counts within that rule.

Stories

Instagram Stories are absurdly fun (and a simple method to lose 60 minutes, doggone!), and at this point, you've most likely had a decent opportunity to play with the Snapchat-esque channels that can transform you into puppies, adorable widdle-bunnies or even a cool ice ruler!

Even though the channels and impacts can like feel even more a curiosity than whatever else, there are awesome advantages to utilizing them deliberately, so to enable you to get your brain around why you require them we're clarifying our five reasons why Instagram Stories should be a piece of your Instagram:

- Instagram Stories are Discoverable.
- 200 million Daily Active Users
- Develop your group
- Advance Exclusivity
- Add a customized way to deal with commitment.

Creating Instagram Stories

Instagram recently added Stories to its Archive feature, allowing users to save their Stories posts within the application after they've expired from public view, as well as to share these posts in Highlights on their profiles. Our guide will show you how to create a Highlight by following some simple steps:

- Step 1: Tap the profile button in the bottom-right corner of the screen.
- Step 2: Tap the + button to begin creating a new Story Highlight.
- Step 3: Scroll through your archive of past Stories posts and tap the circle in the bottom-right corner of each post you wish to add to the Highlight.
- Step 4: When you're done selecting posts, tap "Next."
- Step 5: Type a name for your Highlight.
- Step 6: (optional): Tap "Edit Cover" to change the Highlight's cover image.
- Step 7: Tap "Add" to save the Highlight to your profile.

Best Story Highlights

Curated stories are called "Instagram Stories Highlights," and famous people and brands are already loving this hot new feature. But that's not it! There's also a new Instagram Stories Archive, which automatically saves your Instagram Stories in the cloud, so you don't have to save them to your phone.

Grouping your Instagram Stories Highlights together into various categories, events, or topics makes it super easy for your audience to watch Instagram Stories content that is of specific interest to them. It's also a great way to add value to your feed, explain what your business is about, and attract new Instagram followers with a curated Instagram aesthetic. The key tips related to stories are:

#1: Highlight Place where you are, products or collections

#2: Highlight based on audience or interest

#4: Highlight tutorials or How-to's

#5: Highlight your funs or customers

#6: Highlight your partners & influencers

#7: Highlight your Campaigns

#8: Highlight your events or events that you attend

Adding Your Current Story to a Highlight

You can also add your current story to one of your highlights, as well as use it to create a new highlight altogether. Look at your story by tapping on your profile picture, either in the story row on the feed tab or on your profile picture itself. Then, tap "Highlight" in the bottom-right corner. To add or subtract media from your highlight, long-press on it to bring up the options, then tap "Edit Highlight."

Users in Feed

Instagram is now rearranging users' feeds to show them what it thinks they want to see first rather than showing them all the most recent posts in the order of when they were posted. This algorithm means that you could post something at a particular time and still have it seen by many of your followers or perhaps hardly any of your followers at all, depending on how much or how little they interact with your content.

Time Slots to Post

To figure out your best time to post on Instagram, first take a look at these two major factors that will affect it:

Your target follower demographics: Adults who work the typical 9pm-to-5pm job might be more likely to look at Instagram in the morning, whereas college kids who stay out late and pull all-nighters might be slightly more active on Instagram during those off hours. Identifying your target audience can be a first step toward figuring out what time of day they like to check Instagram.

Time zone differences: If you've got followers or a target audience from all over the world, then posting at specific times of day may not get you the same results as if you had followers who mostly all live around the same time zone. For example, if most of your followers are from North America living in the typical North American time zones of Pacific (PST), Mountain (MST), Central (CST), and Eastern (EST), you could start experimenting with starting to post on Instagram around 7 a.m. EST and stopping around 9 p.m. PST (or 12 a.m. EST). Make sure you pay close attention to any increases in interaction when you post at certain times of day. No matter what the research says or what the experts tell you about optimal time's and days to post, what ultimately matters is the behaviour of your own followers.

Engagement for your posts according to time slot

Iconosquare has an Instagram Analytics feature that will help you understand when to post. Part of its functionality lets you export your data into a spreadsheet where you can see the time you posted and the engagement each post received. As you test you're posting frequency that could be helpful to gauge your engagement by day while analyzing the number of times you posted on Instagram.

Well-known marketing calendar *CoSchedule* collected research from 16 social media studies to come up with these best practices for Instagram:

Mondays and Thursdays drive the most engagement between 3–4 p.m.

Videos any day at 9 p.m.–8 a.m.

Experiment with 2 a.m., 5 p.m., and Wednesday at 7 p.m.

Post Frequency

Post #1: 8–9 a.m.

Post #2: 2 a.m.

Curate and repurpose posts only when necessary (quotes, stats, facts), and always give credit

According to social media management platform *Buffer* major brands share on Instagram on average 1.5 times a day, but not more, so that's also what they suggest you do. Some other experts say to post to Instagram a minimum of three times per day. Since images are super sharable, posting a little more often would be fine, too. A well-known company *Adobe* says your Instagram posting frequency should be consistent with your goals. They say some brands succeed with as many as ten photos per day. That might work well if you're sharing photos from an events, for example.

However, marketing guru Neil Patel disagree by saying that "Posting frequency is not all that important for your Instagram marketing." According to him, what you should focus on is consistency. Whether you post once or twenty times per day, do your best to maintain that same cadence.

Caption

A good Instagram caption is one that provides context, adds personality, and inspires your followers to take action Good Instagram captions come in all shapes and sizes, from short and sweet to a longer, in-depth story (an Instagram caption can be as long as 2200 characters). As long as your audience finds it engaging; you're doing great! Instagram captions give you the opportunity to add context to your photo, or just communicate with your fans, followers and customers! Create your own Instagram voice to go with your brand, and get creative with your caption style.

Creating a call-to-action in your Instagram caption

The simple act of including a call-to-action in your Instagram caption and inviting your audience to comment or engage can go a very long way it when it comes to driving more engagement on your posts.

Using emoji's in your Instagram caption

When you aren't using emoji's to draw attention to your call-to-action, you can use emoji to add personality to your Instagram caption. You can insert multiple emoji at the beginning of your caption to catch the eye of your followers with a bit of color, so they want to click to read more, or you can replace whole words with an emoji.

Good caption examples:

- Watch more sunsets than Netflix.
- Hey, I just met you, this is crazy.
- At least this balloon is attracted to me!
- I must destroy you with hugs and kisses
- Stop looking for happiness in the same place you just lost it.
- I woke up like this.
- I decide the vibe.
- If we could only turn back time…
- Keep smiling because life is a beautiful thing and there's so much to smile about.

Funny Captions:

- Friday, my second favourite F word
- Life isn't perfect. But my Hair is! #selfie addict.
- I didn't choose the thug life, the thug life chose me.
- When I was Rome. I did what the Romans did.

Best Friend Captions:

- I don't know what's tighter, our jeans or our friendship!
- "I would rather walk with a friend in the dark, than alone in the light." —Helen Keller

- Best Friends make good times better and hard times easier!

Use Emoji Effectively:

The wonderful world of emoji's - you either love them or you hate them. But no matter what you feel about them, the reality is that they are dominant in today's communications.

In Your Bio

In my opinion, one of the mandatory places to use emoji's on Instagram, is your bio. I've talked before about the criteria for a good bio, and emoji are a part of this. Your bio is your opportunity to show your personality and style, no matter what that is. Fun, quirky, professional, cute, serious, animal lover, foodie, whatever...

In Your Post Captions

Of course, you can use emoji's in your post captions as well. This is the chance to take your brand personality a little further with each and every post and message you craft.

In Your Comments.

One thing I do a lot is responded to comments with emoji. I use a variety of facial expression emoji for almost every response. And I like to throw in a few other emoji's every now and then too.

Ready For Live

Instagram is going to let everybody around the globe "go live." The organization is extending its live video offering, Instagram Live Stories, to funs and clients around the world. The element will work simply like wherever else: Users can go live by swiping appropriate from their bolsters and choosing live video.

It's been a little more than a year since Instagram enabled us to go live, yet it as of now appears like a basic piece of the online networking stage. Like spilling on Facebook or Twitter, going live on Instagram is an awesome method to interface with devotee's continuously and record your life as it's going on. While going live on Instagram sounds like something that could be an included procedure, it is simple. Contingent upon the fame of your Instagram Live communicate it might appear in the best Instagram Live stories on the Search and Explore tab.

Key advices for live streaming:

- Share situations or stories that teach you life lessons and the most interesting moments. Do not use live too often.
- Live should be thematic. Choose themes for your content. Focus, do not talk about everything. It is boring.
- Question & Answer sessions. Ask questions and give answers is always a good option. People like that.
- Prepare! Some people prepare the whole script, but you don't need to go that far.
- When watching someone go live, there is nothing worse than listening to them ramble without a focus. This broadcasting is serious business! So you want to make sure that your content is legitimate. Imagine that you are preparing for an actual presentation for famous person and customer.

CHAPTER THREE

HASHTAGS ARE YOUR BEST FRIEND

Instagram as of late rolled out an improvement to its calculation, enabling clients to take after hashtags. Stories and posts that utilization the hashtag will be highlighted in a client's newsfeed close by the substance they as of now take after. When clients take after a hashtag, Instagram's calculation should choose which stories to highlight in clients' bolsters in view of an assortment of variables, for example, quality, recency and commitment. Instagram's hashtag calculation is supported by machine-learning innovation, so its underlying rollout may feel somewhat incoherent to a few clients previously the application can figure out which posts are generally important.

While hashtags started on Twitter, they rapidly turned out to be a piece of every online networking channel. Now, Instagram hashtag thickness tends to be significantly more noteworthy than Twitter's since organizations understand the achievement of their Instagram promoting relies upon appropriate hashtagging

How Instagram hashtags work

Each bit of Instagram content you post can be joined by a short message or subtitle and a couple of hashtags. The hashtags help sort out and order pictures and video content, which helps the procedure of substance disclosure and advancement. In addition, Instagram hashtags don't simply remain inside the stage. When somebody shares your Instagram substance to Facebook, the Instagram hashtag is distributed alongside it. This implies your substance has a superior shot of being found by different fans who might not have initially observed the picture or who are scanning for the hashtag with Facebook's Graph Search. This gives a decent method to organizations that have new Instagram records or little adherent numbers to get introduction to more individuals inspired by what they offer.

Hashtag best practices

Regular Instagram clients see hashtags as apparatuses for enhancing the system encounter, though online advertisers see the potential for building groups, expanding brand acknowledgement and broadening business reach.

Entrepreneurs who are new to Instagram tend to commit two errors with regards to utilizing hashtags: utilizing excessively numerous hashtags and utilizing insignificant hashtags. When in doubt, each picture and video your business or you transfers to Instagram ought to incorporate a short inscription. While you can incorporate up to 30 hashtags, consider utilizing close to three to five hashtags. A portion of the main 30 hashtags, for example, #food, and #fashion might be pertinent to your business and are subsequently reasonable diversion. In any case, clients will undoubtedly disregard and even boycott organizations that routinely manhandle and spam hashtags.

Vast organizations that have discovered promoting accomplishment on Instagram utilize prevalent hashtags sparingly they don't indiscriminately apply unimportant hashtags to their substance. Rather, those organizations are more agreeable either commanding hashtags or making new ones that are identified with their brands.

Why you need to use hashtags

The initial step to utilizing hashtags to develop your group of onlookers is to comprehend the way they work on Instagram. When you go into the pursuit highlight of Instagram, you'll see you can seek by top substance, hashtag, individuals (username) and places. Instagram utilizes hashtags to classify content. After you brand your post mutually a hashtag, you'll have a way to press the hashtag to check a page that generally demonstrates told photographs and recordings individuals have transferred mutually that hashtag. When individuals mutually private profiles style posts, they won't disclose up advisedly on hashtag pages. Numbers are permitted in hashtags.

How to grow using hashtags

As already mentioned, Instagram permits up to 30 hashtags with each message. Be that as it may, don't stick 30 hashtags into your post. Rather, consider posting your message with no hashtags. This keeps your post clean and will probably connect with your group of onlookers. After your post is distributed, quickly include hashtags in a remark. The hunt list presents sequentially so looking out for include labels will just purpose them to show up bring down on the hashtag seek.

Studies have demonstrated that posts with at least 11 hashtags get about 80% collaboration, as per marketing guru Neil Patel. In any case, be mindful so as not to utilize very prevalent hashtags. Utilize specialty hashtags spinning around your industry, and farthest point your utilization of hashtags to 15-20 inside a given hour.

Research industry-particular hashtags

A great place in the first place choosing the hashtags that will enable you to come to your Instagram objectives is to find industry-particular hashtags. These are Instagram hashtags that are generally utilized by comparative brands to yours, and by coordinate contenders. You can use these hashtags to help position your substance and your record, and advantage from a prior group.

Contenders' hashtags

To get some motivation for Instagram hashtags you could be utilizing, visit your rivals' Instagram records and check their current posts. What industry-particular hashtags do they utilize that likewise apply to your image? Observe whatever number of these hashtags as could reasonably be expected in a spreadsheet so you can assess them later and utilize the best-fitting ones in your future posts. Remember that prevalent and applicable hashtags change after some time, so it's imperative to invigorate your rundown as frequently as could be allowed.

Brand/Product-related hashtags

Another approach to discover reasonable hashtags is to investigate key terms identifying with your image and item on the Instagram application in 'Labels.' Need some basic hashtag catchphrases to commence your hunt? Look at Hashtag or Rite Tag. These apparatuses let you look scan for general hashtags utilized crosswise over online networking and propose hashtags in view of catchphrases or pictures. Rite Tag has a chrome expansion that gives you a chance to see recommended hashtags for a picture or bit of content just by right-clicking and choosing 'Get Hashtag Suggestions.'

Utilize, long-tail hashtags however much as could reasonably be expected: To ensure your post doesn't lose all sense of direction in an ocean of other comparative posts, you will need to pick hashtags that aren't as of now soaked with related substance. If a hashtag has a great many posts related to it (take #love for instance), I'm sorry to learn, nobody will discover your post through this hashtag.

On the contrary end of the scale, if the hashtags you utilize just have few posts related with them say, not as much as a couple of thousand – it's possible that no one is really hunting down that hashtag because it's as well 'speciality.' When choosing which hashtags will get you the most permeability, and more vitally, draw in the correct gathering of people to your profile, you ought to centre around long-tail hashtags.

Hashtags can truly support your permeability and commitment on Instagram, yet a key approach is fundamental. Inquiring about and reviving your hashtags frequently will guarantee the hashtags you utilize are compelling in helping you develop your record, so keep at it!

Get creative with hashtagging

With regards to utilizing Instagram hashtags, it can be somewhat of a sensitive subject; a few people abhor them, and a few people love them excessively much. Be that as it may, did you realize that posts with no less than one Instagram hashtag normal 12.6% more commitment than posts without a hashtag?

Hashtags (or the new word hashtagging) have turned into a madly well known and powerful approach to impart and discover content by means of online networking. We can surely say that hashtags have impressively developed amid these previous years. The pound image was first made in 1870 and has turned out to be a great deal more imperative today than it at any point was previously. Hashtags now are utilized for labelling and seeking the best online networking locales.

More than that, top organizations around the globe are effectively marking their organization with the hashtag framework once a day. So how would you utilize these hashtags to develop your business or your presence on Instagram? Here are the main five approaches to utilize hashtags.

Nearby hashtag

Social media clients love to post their area with a hashtag and look for individuals with a similar area. For organizations that are privately based, utilizing a nearby hashtag is the ideal approach to pick up introduction through the hashtag framework. Neighborhood labeling will expand sees from indicated neighbourhoods.

Brand name hashtag

The most ideal approach to showcase a brand is by a hashtag! Organizations can expand their image ubiquity and develop their image personality by continually including new posts with their image name hash-labelled. When marking a business mark name, dependably keep it quick and painless.

Drifting items hashtag

Trending things are known to produce the most perspectives and inquiries. At the point when another breaking story emits, it's an awesome plan to include that slanting stories hashtag your post. For bloggers, it is normal to compose blog entries about the following slanting thing so that it will be effortlessly observed.

Catchphrase targeting hashtag

Every business on the web has a watchword focusing on objective. Utilize around three primary catchphrases to dependably hashtag on your online networking profiles. Focusing on your catchphrases through the hashtag framework is a demonstrated method to end up noticeable to significant web-based social networking clients.

On Social Media Today, there has been an investigation that shows out of 74,000,000 tweets, 10.1% of tweets have a hashtag. What does this mean? The hashtag framework is a standout amongst the most effectively utilized online networking labelling frameworks on the web. With such many labels every day, an organization must expand presents and hashtags to keep content crisp and increment sees.

What is good hashtag and where to find quality ones

Instagram is an incredible advertising stage which internet business visionaries can use to help become their web-based business organizations. As we already mentioned – if you to become personally popular on Instagram, you should use all these business techniques on your account. It doesn't make a difference whether you're simply beginning with your store, or in case you're as of now making thousands in income consistently, Instagram is a profitable instrument that you can use further bolstering your good fortune.

When you're utilizing Instagram for your web-based business it's important that you exploit hashtags they are a priceless asset for becoming both your image's span and specialist.

In case you're a continuous online networking client at that point it's possible that you've just observed hashtags in real life.

Instagram hashtags have numerous distinctive purposes here are a couple:

Acquire Likes

Instagram fans and clients who are occupied with a specific field are probably going to look for hashtags which are identified with it. This is the reason it's a smart thought to discover the best Instagram hashtags for likes.

Acquire Followers

Instagram clients who are keen on a specialty are continually searching for more substance that is identified with it. Utilizing the privilege Instagram hashtags is extraordinary compared to other approaches to pick up a higher after on Instagram. It broadens you achieve, empowering your substance to be found, by more individuals.

Make More Sales

Instagram hashtags aren't just about becoming your online business' web-based social networking following. On the off chance that you utilize speciality hashtags while advancing one of your items at that point you're probably going to draw the consideration of clients who are probably going to buy something identified with this substance. This implies you'll have the capacity to support your store's deals with well thoroughly considered Instagram hashtags utilized as a part of mix with convincing substance.

Instructions to find the best Instagram hashtags

Now that we've secured the advantages of utilizing them, it's a great opportunity to clarify how you can locate the best Instagram hashtags for likes. There are a wide range of apparatuses which are accessible which will give you data about the best Instagram Hashtags for likes. It doesn't make a difference what your online store's speciality is, despite everything you'll have the capacity to discover hashtags that are applicable to your substance. Huge numbers of the apparatus are accessible which you can use to create the best Instagram hashtags for likes. Here we will depict the best three apparatuses by which you can get the best Instagram hashtags:

TagBlender is an Instagram hashtag generator instrument that you can use to source hashtags that will convey a high commitment rate to your web-based social networking content.

See metrics is another investigation device which furnishes you with relative measurements to perceive how you are performing close by your rivals.

All Hashtag is a hashtag generator device that enables you to make and investigate the best applicable hashtags by producing many significant hashtags that you would then be able to just reorder your Instagram posts.

Instagram hashtag limit

The Instagram hashtag farthest point may manage your decisions for the Instagram hashtags that you utilize when you're presenting content on your online networking accounts. In case you're utilizing an Instagram hashtag generator to source drawing in hashtags, like the ones specified above, you'll likely get a nonexclusive arrangement of 30 hashtags. In any case, you may find that there are substantially more applicable hashtags for your specific posts.

Tools to find trending hashtags

While social media gives the illusion of complete transparency and thrives (and relies on) user engagement and interaction, it's important for brands to realize that we can still generate and shape social conversations as well as user-created content. One of the best ways to encourage user interaction and content– both of which greatly benefit your brand– is through hashtags.

13 Powerful hashtag tools are as following:

- Hashtagify
- Hootsuite
- Instagram Hashtag Contest Winner Picker
- TINT
- Free Instagram Analytics by TINT
- Talk walker
- RiteTag
- Tweet Chat
- Twitter Advanced Search
- Keyhole
- Mention
- Twubs
- Hashtracking

CHAPTER FOUR

YOU WILL NOT BECOME FAMOUS BY DOING NOTHING

Who wouldn't? Having a lavish existence of venturing to the far corners of the planet, meeting with different renowned and uplifting individuals, being worshipped and the rundown goes on. Sounds great isn't that right? Well to end up popular on Instagram or some other web-based social networking stage is not something you set yourself out to do – or is it?

Particularly by doing nothing, you can't be being well known on Instagram. It doesn't generally make a difference to what extent it takes. On the off chance that you need it enough, you can accomplish this. The world truly is your clam.

In any case, I accept there are sure prescribed procedures that assist you to end up popular on Instagram. As an Instagram showcasing master, I've assembled this article to help everybody get into the spotlight speedier.

Do you need your image to contact a greater gathering of people? Would you like it to be a prevalent name in web-based social networking? Is it true that you are searching for a considerably greater and better place to feature your one of a kind items and administrations?

Welcome to the universe of Instagrama massively innovative and drawing in stage where you can associate with a large number of clients and advance your image successfully. With just about 70% of brands over the world finding better approaches to draw in with the Instagram people group, the opportunity has already come and gone your image went with the same pattern.

Instagram's ubiquity has been developing relentlessly since it initially appeared in 2010. Within excess of 500 million dynamic users, it's at present the second most prevalent web-based social networking system on the planet, behind just Facebook (unless you check YouTube), and advertisers are falling more enamoured with the stage.

Truth be told, the quantity of sponsors on Instagram has multiplied in the course of recent months or somewhere in the vicinity, to in excess of one million, to some extent because of the way that Instagram is presently viewed as the best online networking stage for client commitment. In any case, would it be that makes the stage so captivating to clients, and by what method would marketer's be able to exploit it? They can be your sponsor too!

According to *Metrics,* "commitment" is difficult to gauge, and includes a few variables, like post permeability, inclination to remark, and shareability. But basically, it's your capacity to associate with your devotees. In an overview of more than 2,500 smaller scale influencers (average sized online networking clients with a huge after of every day drew in clients), 60 percent thought Instagram was the best general stage for commitment. The sprinter up, Facebook, just accumulated help of 18 percent. So why is Instagram so great at drawing in with gatherings of people?

Instagram is additionally a takeoff from applications like Facebook, Twitter, and LinkedIn, for the most part, due to its straightforwardness. It's completed an extraordinary activity of drawing in more youthful gatherings of people, with the lion's share of its clients checking in at under age 30 and has a vitality that more seasoned online networking brands have lost throughout the years.

There are numerous organizations which propose getting Instagram adherents for your record quickly and successfully. In this section, we will depict how to do it with no rush and keeping high calibre of your supporters.

Get Local

With a specific end goal to get genuine nearby supporters independent from anyone else, not utilizing different administrations, you ought to comprehend for what reasons for existing are you going to utilize your Instagram account:

- For simply gathering private pictures and imparting them to companions. Here the measure of supporters does not assume any part.
- For attention. If you are a media identity or you want to be famous, the more supporters you have, the better it is.
- In business implies for the reasons for marking. Accumulate your assembly hall and lift the unmistakable quality of your image.

When you have characterized your motivation, begin breathing life into it. Unmistakably with a specific end goal to gather live supporters, one has to post intriguing photographs (or possibly felines), however, we've gathered some specialized advice to help you in your battle.

Call Others For Action

Toward the finish of most business-related Instagram posts, you'll see an incredible activity guiding guests to accomplish something next like "Tap the connection." In advertising, this is known as the "Suggestion to take action." Invitations to act (CTAs) have the part of coordinating individuals into what they ought to do straight away. You can request that they purchase your item, visit your site or connect with you. In any case, not all CTAs are the same. The key is to be as innovative as you can be keeping in mind the end goal to influence individuals to make a move.

Like any change to your web-based social networking approach, we propose you have a go at testing new forms to see which one connects with your clients the most. Here are five imaginative, fascinating and usable suggestions to take action that you can use on your next post:

- Bother your followers
- Give the audience a chance to see the need
- Urge followers to tag their friends
- Utilize active language
- Make a sense of urgency

When it comes time to settle on a buying choice, who are you more prone to trust - a brand, or a kindred customer who utilizes the item? Will probably take proposals from loved ones than brands when it comes time to settle on purchasing choices - and that is the rationale behind client produced content via web-based networking media.

Client created substance (UGC) comprises of any type of substance that is made by clients and purchasers about a brand or item. UGC isn't paid for, and its validness makes the client the brand promoter too. UGC is especially predominant on Instagram, where brands can without much of a stretch repost and regard UGC from clients' records. Furthermore, it's beneficial for brands to do this - 76% of people reviewed said they trusted substance shared by "normal" individuals more than by brands, and about 100% of purchasers confide in proposals from others.

Programming goliath *IBM* utilizes UGC on Instagram fundamentally from its clients and group individuals utilizing the hashtag #IBM. Its UGC procedure is easier than some depicted already, yet it completes an awesome activity at giving an inside take a gander at one of the greatest innovation organizations on the planet. Auto-organization BMW utilizes #BMWRepost to share Instagram posts of pleased BMW proprietors and their wheels. BMW pitches extravagance autos to proprietors who are without a doubt glad for their accomplishment, and this crusade gives proprietors the chance to flaunt - and gives BMW a chance to flaunt its pleased and faithful base of clients.

Collaborate with others

I see numerous organizations dither to work together with bloggers and brand influencers on Instagram claiming they don't know how to go about it. I have a couple of (fruitful!) coordinated efforts added to my repertoire and scholarly the intricate details of working with a blogger or brand influencer for a cooperation on Instagram. What's more, given me a chance to reveal to you something: everyone can change. Since every blogger works their business distinctively as far as picking and styling items, posting on Instagram, and obviously, the loved and admired subject, instalment, that implies every cooperation can contrast. The nuts and bolts of teaming up with a blogger or brand influencer that stay the same. Teaming up with a blogger or brand influencer doesn't need to be troublesome.

Four Easy Steps To Collaborating On Instagram

- *Discover a blogger or brand influencer you need to work with:* You must pick somebody that functions admirably with your items and your business. Take an hour to stay nearby on Instagram and see who you might want to work together with. Ensure their style and identity would work well with your image.
- *The number of adherents you have mattered:* When searching for bloggers or brand influencers to work with, you have to ensure their style and identity will work with your image and that you have a comparable measure of devotees.
- *Contact the blogger or brand influencer:* You are endeavouring to wrap up a business bargain and a business bargain is somewhat proficient, so a joint effort demand ought to get through an expert email address.
- *Settle on the points of interest of your joint effort and work together:* It all begins with the sorts of items the brand influencer will get are there set items set up that should be advanced or does the blogger get the chance to pick what they might want to include?

Square away every one of the points of interest from the items to the Instagram presents on pay. Your joint effort will run smoother if you escape most importantly. My four-stage procedure to working together with a blogger or brand influencer is somewhat straightforward. When we spoke before about hashing out every one of the points of interest of the coordinated effort, a standout amongst the most vital parts of the cooperation is making sense of already what kind you need to have.

Engage Your Fans

During the most recent three years, Instagram has advanced from a place to post photographs of your nourishment to a capable driver of business for a portion of the greatest brands on the planet. Reception among web clients and organizations has detonated and, not at all like on most other informal communities, individuals tend to fill their Instagram encourages with mark content. Truth be told, as per marketing research company *Forrester*, Instagram has the most astounding commitment rates amongst brands and clients contrasted with other significant informal communities.

An informal community where individuals really need organizations to get included sounds like a blessing from heaven, yet doesn't underestimate that receptiveness. Your fans anticipate that you will treat Instagram simply like they would: filling you encourage with delightful pictures, remarking on the photographs of others, and for the most part being locks in. In case you don't know how to draw in your crowd past preferences and remarks, we've accumulated a modest bunch of different strategies to truly establish a connection on Instagram.

Utilize influencers

If you're hoping to expand your permeability, consider connecting with other compelling Instagram clients and records. Nowadays, online networking influencers resemble current superstars. Teaming up with influencers will help build you achieve, image mindfulness, and show individuals that you're focusing on patterns.

Utilize regramming

One of the most intense approaches to draw in your Instagram adherents is to swing to them for client created content. Regramming the act of posting a photograph from another person's Instagram record to your own, alongside fitting credit is one of the least demanding and best methods for drawing in your gathering of people.

The photograph's maker gets an individual yell out from a brand and expanded presentation through their system. As a brand, you demonstrate to your group of onlookers that you're focusing on them and will share their substance.

Utilize your inscriptions

Excessively numerous brands regard the Instagram subtitle as an idea in retrospect. Truly, Instagram is a visual informal organization and the photographs matter most, however, your subtitle is profitable land that you can use to provoke advance commitment. A decent subtitle trust it or not, most likely won't be only a couple of words. The best Instagrammers on the planet tend to recount a story, make an inquiry or utilize fun hashtags or emoticons. Investing energy precisely making the ideal inscription will breathe life into your picture and enable your devotees to identify with you and your substance.

Partake in your remark strings

Observing what your adherents are saying in regard to the photographs you post, both positive and negative is a major piece of connecting with your gathering of people. Thank individuals for kind remarks or for labelling their companions. All things considered react to remarks where individuals get some information about the photograph, or about your business.

Run challenges and battles

Facilitating a challenge can construct some genuine fervour around your business or brand. Instagram really makes it entirely simple to run speedy challenges that will construct your following and increment commitment. Remark challenges request that supporters do somewhat more work, by remarking on your photograph with a specific end goal to participate in the challenge. These challenges are regularly confined as "disclose to us why you need to win this prize" or "label three of your companions."

CHAPTER FIVE

WHEN AND HOW TO USE INSTAGRAM?

Instagram is one of the most blazing interpersonal organizations now. It's visual, it's snappy, it's versatile and it's entirely easy to utilize. There's no preferable time over now, to begin with Instagram. The accompanying seven reminders can enable you when you to make the best out of your own Instagram encounter with the goal that you can develop your supporters and increment commitment.:

- Post Interesting, Colorful Photos and Videos
- Do whatever it takes Not to Overdo It with the Filter Effects
- Utilize Hashtags Sparingly
- Utilize the Explore Tab (Popular Page) to Find Great New Content
- Post Often to Keep Followers Interested
- Utilize Instagram Direct to Contact Specific Users
- Associate with Your Followers

Develop own Instagram style

Need your Instagram bolster to mirror your image? Searching for approaches to make an Instagram nearness individual perceive? Pulling in your intended interest group on Instagram begins with an all-around arranged way to deal with your visuals. And this segment, you'll find how to build up your own Instagram style.

Reverberate your brand's visual identity

Brand resources like textual styles, hues, and logos are essential instruments for making brand acknowledgement and review. Utilize your advantages reliably, and your adherents can recognize your posts all the more effortlessly in the encourage.

Pick a signature filter

One of the most straightforward approaches to minister your Instagram nourish and make a durable tasteful is to locate the correct channel and stay with it. Although that doesn't mean you need to stay with a solitary channel for whatever remains of your Instagram marking life, it means constraining yourself to a couple of comparable channels.

Offer How-to content

Using channels isn't the best way to be imaginative with your photographs on Instagram. There are numerous other intriguing approaches to connect with your photography! Photograph collections, for instance, are a fun method to highlight numerous pictures in a solitary post. They're outwardly powerful and amazingly valuable for visual substance showcasing.

Highlight product images from your fans

Social media is tied in with being associated with your group of onlookers, and nothing completes a superior employment of that than client created content. These kinds of Instagram posts are imperative for two reasons. In the first place, they divert your Instagram nourish from a handout like collection into a natural and bona fide narrating vehicle. Second, they change your group of onlookers into a group.

To effectively market to your group of onlookers on a visual stage, for example, Instagram, you have to build up an immediately conspicuous nearness. From your general nourish to the individual pictures and recordings you post, everyone ought to fortify brand review. Utilize the tips above to enable you to make an Instagram sustain that draws in supporters, as well as mirrors your business picture.

Post At Your Best Times

The best circumstances to post via web-based networking media are the point at which the general population you need to see the substance are on the system. There are best practices for every informal community will enable you to get more movement, greater commitment, and more supporters. The best time to post on Instagram is 2 a.m. also, 5 p.m. The pinnacle time and day is Wednesday at seven p.m. Here is some advice from experts in this field:

TrackMaven: The best time to post recordings is between 9 p.m.– 8 a.m. with picture posts reliable during the time with slight tops on Thursday and Monday.

Brisk Sprout: Instagram commitment is genuinely unfaltering, with slight increments on Monday and abatements on Sunday. In general, however, anytime is great. As indicated by Patel, who noticed that weekday commitment was genuinely comparable, the same could be said for time of day. Most Instagram clients draw in with Instagram content more amid off-work hours than amid the workday.

Elle and Co.: The greatest day to post on Instagram is Monday. Posting for the duration of the day would be fine since Instagram clients are reliably dynamic. Be that as it may, there is a slight dunk in movement from 3– 4 p.m.

Huffington Post: The best time to post on Instagram is two a.m. furthermore, 5p.m. The pinnacle time and day is Wednesday at 7p.m.

TrackMaven: The best time to post recordings is between 9p.m.–8a.m. with picture posts predictable during the time with slight tops on Thursday and Monday.

MarketingProfs: Posting on Instagram between 1– 2 p.m. is best for commitment. Monday is an awesome day to help your commitment, and particularly from 8– 9 a.m. Afterwards, avoid posting amid work hours, particularly between 3 p.m.

CoSchedule: Sadly, it's extremely difficult to get movement from Instagram. In any case, if that is your objective, attempt Tuesdays at 2 p.m. Iconosquare is an Instagram investigation apparatus that has an element to enable you to comprehend when to post to Instagram to achieve your very own greater amount adherents.

Attract More And More Followers

Instagram rapidly exceeded its early introduction as a fun application for kids and has turned into a genuine substance advertising, systems administration and gathering of people building an instrument for people and brands. It's a standout amongst the most well-known long range informal communication destinations on the planet, with more than 200 million dynamic months to month individuals sharing 60 million pictures and 1.6 billion preferences for each day.

Exactly how great is it? Commitment rates for brands on most informal communities are under 0.1%, however, Instagram overwhelms them all. The normal Instagram commitment rate for brands in a 2014 Forrester think about was an epic 58 times higher than on Facebook.

Of course, 58 times more prominent commitment than Facebook sounds awesome, however, you can do as such much superior to that on Instagram. Regardless of whether you're a major brand or perhaps simply considering how to end up Instagram acclaimed, I don't need you to take a stab at normal; I need you to try to achieve the impossible and turn into an Instagram unicorn. An advanced unicorn is that supernatural, uncommon animal that beats all others by requests of greatness.

Cross-advance your committed hashtag

That is decent that you made a #joesgarage hashtag for your organization, however, who knows to utilize it to share content about you? Ensure it's in your profile, however, take the diversion disconnected and have it imprinted on your receipts, in print promotions, on signage in your store and at important occasions.

Get inventive with hashtagging

With regards to Instagram subtitle thoughts, you have to look past the single word, evident hashtags (see above). Without a doubt, you need to utilize those, as well, however, blend it up and utilize hashtags to recount some portion of your story.

Participate in greatly well-known discussions

For each post, utilize a blend of topically pertinent hashtags, for example, #woodworking for a carpentry organization, for instance, and in addition slanting, super-prevalent hashtags wherever you can.

Get distinct with your subtitles

Words generally can't do a picture justice; however, you can't skirt the words altogether. National Geographic is awesome at utilizing narrating close by their Instagram photographs to create commitment and sharing.

Approve photograph labels before the substance appears on your profile

Discussing gives you more prominent control over which labelled photographs show up on your profile, you can change your Instagram setting so labelled photographs won't demonstrate unless you support them first. You'll locate this under "Alternatives," "Photographs of You," and "Include Manually."

Should I Follow A Lot Or Not?

Instagram is about connections and the general population you take after ought to be a piece of that want to fabricate connections. I need to begin by saying that you ought to take a "decent" number of individuals. There is no flawless proportion or normal that I can exhort you on. Be that as it may, on the off chance that you have 1000 devotees and just take ten individuals, that doesn't look great. If you have 10,000 adherents and take 200 individuals, that likewise doesn't look so great.

I unquestionably prescribe you take after no less than 100 individuals. Get yourself out there and drawing in with others. You can't do that lone after 50 individuals. Here are some great rules to consider for who to take after on Instagram.

Take after those who interest you

This is the greatest and most essential tip. Take after the individuals who intrigue you. Take after organizations, brands, big names, picture takers, artisans, charming creatures, and specialists. On the off chance that they share content you appreciate then you ought to tail them. Take after your companions, family, and individuals you've met. If they are individuals you need to remain associated with, at that pointed tail them.

Signup with Facebook

This is the easiest and quickest way to set up your Instagram account. It will automatically allow you to follow your friends that are already on Instagram and in turn; they will follow you too. Your friends and family will be the first followers on Instagram which will help boost your profile and get you ready for the main deal.

Take after the good examples

I exceptionally suggest you discover organizations and brands in your industry and different businesses who are utilizing Instagram well. At that point tail them. This is particularly imperative when you initially begin on Instagram. It's vital that you perceive how others are utilizing Instagram and why. Be specific in who you take after on Instagram. Since the nourish demonstrates to all of you of everybody's substance, you will have bounty to take a gander at. What's more, don't be hesitant to unfollow somebody not far off.

Like other photos a lot

This is a good thing if you do. It helps you make relationships with those people who are unknown for you but can be beneficial for you. But you should like the photos of only those people who post valuable photos. Now we talk about how we can get a lot of likes on our feed on Instagram.

Exchange shoutouts

This is simply a method of promoting others while they promote you too. It's simply a win-win situation for both members. This method helps in promoting your profile. You need to simply find people within your niche and reach out to them and ask for a shoutout. You can do this by sending them a simple email or request on Instagram.

Instagram is a splendid method to impart recollections and most loved minutes to companions, family, and irregular devotees. In case you're posting a lot of photographs, but not accepting the same number of preferences as you need, take after these basic strides to get more likes.

- Begin loving the photographs of irregular individuals to get more like back.
- Utilize hashtags to sort photographs with watchwords.
- Use however many hashtags as would be prudent for every photograph.
- Utilize the most famous hashtags (oh, hashtags again)
- Pursuit the rundown of slanting hashtags and utilize one of them
- Apply channels to your photographs.
- Utilize the applications on your telephone to make photographs engaging and exceptional

- Post the privilege photographs.
- Post the best individual photographs that show you with your life partner, companions, and relatives.
- Post photographs of novel perspectives.
- Be a dynamic individual from the Instagram people group to get likes and remarks.
- Post photographs at the perfect time. As we have specified in above

Thusly, it's a decent trap to wind up acclaimed on Instagram. Simply like others photographs a great deal.

Be positive

Now and again web-based social networking gets an awful notoriety and that is justifiable. Instagram, Facebook, Twitter, YouTube and other web-based social networking destinations have succumbed to tormenting, badgering, judgment, "Facebook battles," and so on. Although there are strategies against these kinds of things, it's unavoidable. As people were obstinate and some of the time our conclusions conflict with everyone around us. Some of the time we act in way that isn't precisely proper. This is when web-based social networking can turn appalling.

We're not continually going to concur with everyone around us, and it appears that is an extreme pill to swallow. As opposed to reviewing online networking as a hatchery for issues, we should utilize it emphatically. Here's a rundown of things we could do to make web-based social networking a positive and well-disposed condition:

- Spread love, support, and consolation
- Associate with loved ones

- Offer individual objectives, qualities, achievements, stories, and so forth.
- Give and offer exhortation and proposal
- Instruct and educate yourself as well as other people
- Offer photograph, images and clever recordings for a decent chuckle
- Take after and share rousing records
- Bring issues to light for an association that you adore

Keep in mind what your mother dependably let you know (the brilliant administers, "in the event that you don't have anything decent to state, don't state anything by any means"). In conclusion, reconsider before you click 'Post,' 'Tweet,' and so forth.

Organize contests for followers

Common Instagram contest mechanics:

- To enter an Instagram contest you usually have to follow the account posting the contest.
- Entrants are usually required to like the contest post
- Entrants are usually required to @ mention another Instagram user in the comments. Often each @ mention counts as an additional contest entry

The vast majority of Instagram contests in our study used variations on these common contest mechanics. However there's nothing from stopping you getting creative, as long as you abide by Instagram's Promotion Guidelines. These include a requirement to include "Acknowledgement that the promotion is in no way sponsored, endorsed or administered by, or associated with, Instagram."

Other types of Instagram contests include:

- Like to enter (double-tap to win)
- Photo contests (post your entrance with this branded hashtag)
- In-store contests (take a photo inside our store and post it with this branded hashtag)

Ideas for Instagram contests

Instagram contests give people an entertaining reason to interact with and promote your business and products.

Host a like-to-win contest

One major factor in finding success on Instagram is getting those magic likes to start rolling in. A "like to win" contest is an easy way to do that. Simply post a contest image (usually a graphic explaining the contest) and tell people to like it to win. Then pick a random winner from among the likes, comment with the winner's handle, and boom, you've created a contest.

Launch a selfie contest

In a selfie contest, you invite people to post photos of them using your product, posing in unique locations, or showing off your logo all over the city. Selfie contests on Instagram do a wonderful job of connecting your audience to your product and putting social context around your marketing. There's no better example of personal engagement with a product than through a selfie contest.

Run a hashtag contest

Like so much of social media, Instagram is built on hashtags. In a hashtag contest, ask people to post photos and require they use your hashtag. Then you just search for the hashtag and choose the winner.

CHAPTER SIX

DO I NEED EXTERNAL HELP WHILE USING INSTAGRAM?

Here, outside help implies alternate records which use for business point of view and connected to Instagram. Instagram may require no presentation, yet for the new, it is a free person to person communication application that gives clients a chance to catch and offer photographs and recordings. Since Instagram is a standout amongst the most prominent social applications, you might need to interface most of your social records to receive the most in return. You can interface your Twitter, Facebook, Tumblr, and Flickr accounts; there are additionally less-well-known systems (in the United States, at any rate) that you can connect to, including Ameba. You may need to hire external help to deal with your account or professional photographer to make the most fantastic photos for your profile.

Exchanging Between Accounts

To switch between your records, backpedal to your profile and tap on your client name at the upper left to raise a menu of introduced accounts. Select the one you wish to utilize, and the application will switch accounts. You additionally have the alternative of including another record straightforwardly from this menu.

This is an extremely welcome and long past due move from Instagram. The simplicity of exchanging records ought to urge multi-account clients to end up more dynamic on the administration, while those with only one record may feel urged to include more now that the procedure has turned out to be inconsequentially simple.

Buying Followers – Yes Or Not

You could become your Instagram following the legit way— creating an insightful technique, defining shrewd objectives, sharing incredible substance, and connecting with your crowd. Or on the other hand, you could take the brisk and simple way and join the dull side of Instagram advertising. You could purchase Instagram devotees.

Why should I purchase Instagram devotees?

Brands, superstars, influencers, and even lawmakers have been known to cushion their online networking details by including counterfeit supporters.

For what reason do they do it?

It's about recognition. The quantity of adherents is something that numerous individuals take a gander at when surveying a record to take after and it's a typical metric that brands use to gauge their own Instagram endeavours.

In case you're considering purchasing Instagram supporters, it may be on account of you're searching for a brisk thousand adherents to take care of business, trusting that will urge genuine individuals to look at your image. Quality over amount is a pleasant opinion, however, actually, numerous individuals judge an Instagram account by its numbers. Additionally, purchasing Instagram adherents is shabby and simple to do, as you're going to learn.

How Purchasing Instagram Devotees Functions?

In the first place, it's critical to take note of the refinement we're making here between the express demonstration of purchasing devotees and the all the more approximately characterized routine with regards to Instagram computerization. Buying Instagram supporters is against Instagram rules, and many experts see this action as a big waste of money and time.

Instagram mechanization can allude to the demonstration of enabling a bot to like and remark for your sake. On the off chance that you'd get a kick out of the chance to take in more about that not recommended easy route. Purchasing adherents on Instagram, then again, is precisely that. You connect your record to an administration, make installment, and watch your group of onlookers develop.

It can be very shoddy, with numerous administrations charging around USD3 for every 100 supporters. In any case, you get what you pay for. By and large, that is bots and zombie accounts (inert records that have been assumed control by bots).

There are additionally more costly choices that charge upwards of $1,000 for 10,000 adherents. Those administrations keep up dynamic records that will interface with your own.

A few instruments will take after clients for your benefit in the expectations that they give back where its due. You'll be solicited what kind from accounts you need to take after in view of things, for example, area, hashtag utilization, comparative records, and sexual orientation. At that point, after a foreordained time, the bot unfollows anybody that didn't tail you back.

The Instagram adherent apparatus we explored different avenues regarding didn't do any of that. Truth be told, our spurious record has never tailed anybody but or genuine client.

Why you shouldn't purchase instagram supporters?

You get what you pay for: a number. This supporters won't care for any of your posts and they won't leave any remarks. Also, you risk getting captured. Regardless of whether you have honest to goodness fans, anybody investigating your devotee rundown may detect an extent of phoney and inert records.

When you take easy routes, you put your image trustworthiness in danger. In the event that you purchase Instagram adherents and your genuine clients discover, would you be able to anticipate that they will believe you?

Professional Photographer?

Within excess of 600 million month to month dynamic clients, Instagram offers awesome open doors for picture takers to manufacture a group of people of devoted fans. In any case, persuading a million of those individuals to tail you is an accomplishment by and large saved for hotshots, brands and a modest bunch of influencers. It is a question of money, time and taste if you will ask some professional photographer to make your photo. Quite often, they will accept the cooperation even without money. In the end, you will promote their work, and they will give you fantastic photos.

With a couple of very much utilized traps and fantastic photography aptitudes, these five picture takers have figured out how to approach and even surpass that stamp. Here is how they did it and what they have realized in route.:

- Chris Burkard (2,300.000): Four years back, Chris Burkard was on an excursion in Iceland (he has been there 27 times) shooting surfers when one of them acquainted him with Instagram. His work is covering sports and outside enterprise centers around catching the instinctive experience of heading off to the spots he shoots.
- David Guttenfelder (987.000): A substantial after came effortlessly to David Guttenfelder. As the main Asia picture taker for the Associated Press, he was positioned in North Korea from 2011 to 2014. While there, he could give exceptional visual access to a nation shut off toward the West. An exceptionally granted picture taker, Guttenfelder was less inspired with what his Instagram following improved the situation his profession than what it improved the situation his photography.
- Pei Ketron (830.000): Pei Ketron lives in San Francisco and began posting on Instagram in October 2010, just seven days after it propelled.
- Jimmy Chin (1,500.000) Jimmy Chin was an eminent picture taker a long time before he opened a record on Instagram.
- Murad Osmann (4,500.000): Osmann went for a creative organization and keeping in mind that his companions were irritated by the monotonous idea of his bolster, achievement came eighteen months after the fact when it was posted on Reddit.

Instagram is an undeniable place to head yet how would you deal with the billions of normal pictures to discover the jewels in the unpleasant? Indeed, one you think can do is to take the privilege Instagram clients. Here we've chosen a couple of incredible records to take after to kick you off.:

- Simone Bramante: Simone Bramante catches mystical scene symbolism, frequently highlighting human subjects
- Victoria Siemer: Victoria Siemer has a conceptual style with powerful hints. The picture taker – who passes by the name of Witchoria – has piled on thousands of adherents with her barometrical pictures.
- Dirk Bakker: Dirk Bakker is a visual fashioner and picture taken with an eye for engineering designs. His arrangements will drive you to see the scene in an unexpected way.
- Janske Kaethoven: For forlorn scenes and a solid measurement of nature, look no more remote than Kaethoven. Tremendous seascapes sit nearby creature representations in this differed Instagram account.
- Asa Sjostrom: Asa Sjostrom has an emphasis on social issues, particularly concerning ladies and kids. "As a photojournalist, I need to make mindfulness and make progress toward hint circumstances amongst me and the general population in my photos," she says on her portfolio site.
- Dave Yoder: Dave Yoder is a normal benefactor, which implies his Instagram nourish is frequently brimming with motivational, shrewd and extremely rather wonderful symbolism. Displaying happenings from each side of the world, Yoder's record ought to be first on your 'take after' rundown.
- Theron Humphrey: heron Humphrey's adorable pooch Maddie truly influenced this one for us. Be that as it may, regardless of whether you're a creature sweetheart or not, Humphrey's capacity to catch minutes like this is genuinely rousing. He's likewise won National Geographic's Traveler of the Year Award.

- Mike Kus: Mike Kus was one of the principal creators to begin utilizing Instagram, and it appears in the mind-blowing measure of devotees he's amassed. Cases of tasks he's posted on the application incorporate a backstage shoot for Burberry at London form week and an accumulation of shots from Sicily for O2.

I strongly suggest contacting some of those people or other photographers that you may like. You have nothing to lose, and you may get best even photos of yourself. Maybe you won't be able to work with listed ones, but some rising star will help you on your way to becoming famous on Instagram.

CONCLUSION

Today, most of our social collaborations are mixed with visuals snapping a brisk photograph to content to a companion, posturing at a bar for a selfie, or killing a couple of minutes looking over newsfeeds loaded with photographs and recordings. The effect of the ascent of visual substance on interpersonal organizations is most clear on Instagram. Thus, numerous brands are scrambling to see how to best utilize Instagram benefits.

It's imperative to recognize and investigate your overall computerized design and decide if Instagram is a solid match for your gathering of people. From that point, it's a great opportunity to design. Instagram is likewise bouncing locally available to help advertisers. These tips and traps will help you in the arranging stages, yet continually drive yourself to be imaginative and think extraordinary. Try to make convincing substance and decline to acknowledge the conviction that what others have done in the past must be imitated. Endeavour to make your way and utilize Instagram to outwardly draw in and associate with your group of onlookers.

Through this "investigation" of Instagram and the itemized examination of each element, we can not just see how Instagram fills in as a helpful and viable path for standard individuals to make and offer their own stories carefully, it's unquestionably workable for individuals'. Instagram records to be irregular "disorders of data" or non-durable information focuses simply like Facebook notices offer no rational account, the shape and the highlights of Instagram plainly encourage narrating and make it simple for individuals to ponder their lives and select the stories they need to share. Most importantly, computerized narrating through Instagram works since individuals trust that there is significance in regular day to day existence they needn't bother with a colossal occasion to impart to the world

As things are ending up progressively versatile and productive, an application like Instagram is the ideal path for individuals to alter their own photographs in a hurry. The social part of the application is another key component that our intended interest group searches for, the sharing highlights on Instagram is the entire method to share your photographs with your loved ones on your different online networking destinations. Instagram enables its clients to draw in with different clients and communicate their energizing lifetime minutes to the innovative world. These two ideas are imperative to the present youth.

Utilizing Instagram on your site enables you to interface with funs and clients over various channels and increment cross-channel commitment. Instagram drives more connected with activity than some other social channel. Instagram has the potential for client created content implicit. You never need to put officially tight Instagram assets in content that won't perform well. Fortunately, on Instagram, you as of now have input about how your crowd will respond to content before you take up important land on your site or spend cash for Instagram advertisements.

Hope you will become famous on Instagram soon!

ABOUT THE AUTHOR

Susan Howard (born 1979) is an American writer, performer, and social media expert, born and raised in Los Angeles, who lives and works in New York. Her writing includes mostly blogs, articles, and ebooks related to social media, modern living and urban life. She is focused on practical support to young generations, explaining modern phenomena on the most understandable way to help people to achieve a better life in different aspects.

ONE LAST THING

If you enjoyed this book or found it useful, I'd be very grateful if you'd post a short review on Amazon. Your support does make a difference, and I read all the reviews personally, so I can get your feedback and make this book even better.

Thanks again for your support!

Please send me your feedback at
www.urbanlife.tips

35578418R00040

Printed in Poland
by Amazon Fulfillment
Poland Sp. z o.o., Wrocław